CANDLE IN THE WIND

ELTON JOHN & BERNIE TAUPIN

NEW YORK

Goodbye
Norma Jean,

Though I never knew you at all

Though I never knew you at all

You had the grace to hold yourself

While those around you crawled.

They crawled out of the woodwork,
And they whispered into your brain,

They set you on the treadmill

And they made you change your name.

And it seems to me you lived your life
Like a candle in the wind.

Never knowing who to cling to

When the rain set in.

And I would have liked to have known you

But I was just a kid.

Your candle burned out
long before
Your legend ever did.

Loneliness was tough,
The toughest role you ever played.

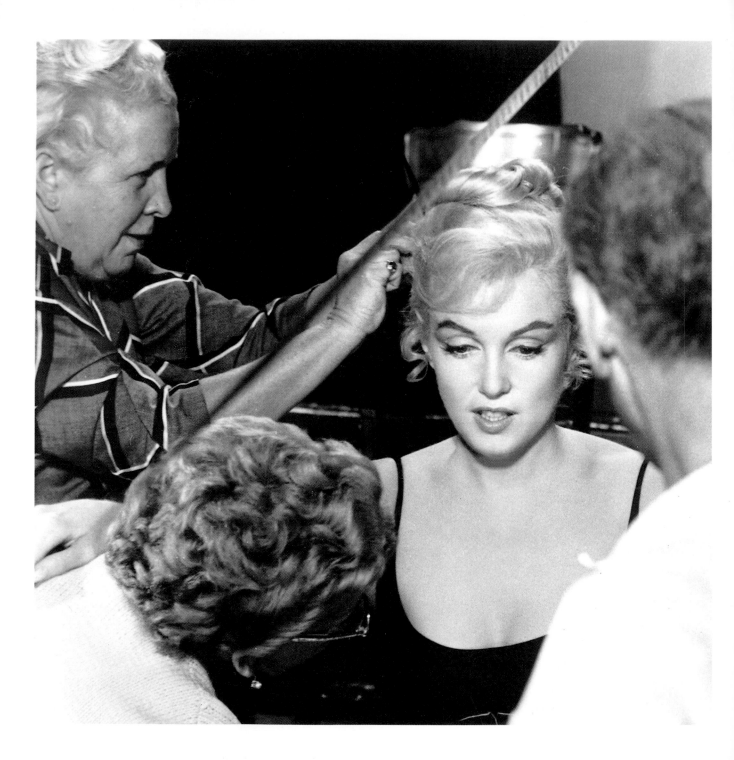

Hollywood created a superstar

And pain was the price you paid.

Even when you died

The press still hounded you

All the papers had to say

Was that Marilyn was found in the nude.

Goodbye Norma Jean,

Though I never knew you at all

You had the grace to hold yourself

While those around you crawled.

Goodbye Norma Jean,
        From the young man in the 22nd row

Who sees you as something more than sexual,
More than just our
Marilyn Monroe.

Candle in the Wind © 1973 written by Elton John & Bernie Taupin
Published by Dick James Music/Polygram Music Publishing Ltd.

Designed by Wherefore Art?
Additional photography by Dan Einzig

For information address:
Hyperion, 114 Fifth Avenue
New York, New York 10011

ISBN 0-7868-6000-6

FIRST EDITION

Printed and bound in China by Imago

10 9 8 7 6 5 4 3 2 1

Acknowledgements

The publishers wish to thank the following copyright holders
for their permission to reproduce illustrations supplied:

p.5 Milton H. Greene, ©1974 Milton H. Greene Trust

from the Private Collection of Joshua and Anthony Greene

p.7 Andre de Dienes, ©1993 de Dienes Photographic Arts

pp.8, 10, 16, 17, 22, 23, 25, 26, 27, 28, 32 courtesy of the Kobal Collection

pp.12, 15, 19, 21, trace page 24/25, 29 courtesy of the Hulton Deutsch Collection

pp.9, trace page 32/33 Sam Shaw, ©1993 Larry Shaw

p.20 Associated Press

p.31 Bob Henriques, Magnum Photos

pp.35, 40 Eve Arnold, Magnum Photos

p.36 Inge Morath, Magnum Photos

p.39 Burt Glinn, Magnum Photos

p.43 Bert Stern ©1993